Intuition and The New Age

Intuition and The New Age

A Treatise on Yoga and Self Realization

Robert L. Crosman

authorHOUSE®

AuthorHouse™
1663 Liberty Drive
Bloomington, IN 47403
www.authorhouse.com
Phone: 1-800-839-8640

First published by AuthorHouse   11/03/2011

ISBN: 978-1-4670-6265-7 (sc)
ISBN: 978-1-4670-6264-0 (ebk)

Library of Congress Control Number: 2011918364

Printed in the United States of America

INTUITION AND THE NEW AGE

Introduction

"So what's your next move?"

"I'm going to write a book. I figure as long as I'm hanging out with a publisher I might as well write a book"

"Um . . . Even though I don't publish books . . ."

"You're going to. You're going to publish this one and make some extra money."

"Well . . . what's it called?""

"It's called "*Intuition and the New Age*" (laughs)

"I'm not laughing . . ."

"I am laughing . . ."

"Why?"

"I don't know why really. I'd like to be serious about it. I always thought I would write a book and now I have to. Well, I don't really have to . . ."

"What's it about?"

"Intuition and the New Age. It's about what's behind the human search for meaning. What compels human beings to search for physical security and, beyond that why we're rarely at peace with ourselves and always looking for something more. What is the 'more' that human beings are searching for? What's the reason for having religion, science and psychology? So, if you look at it, human beings have always had 'spiritual' aspirations. There's something to know, something to realize. I've been involved in it my entire adult life."

"Would you interview people?"

"You"

"Me?'

"You're my favorite guinea pig."

"No, I mean for the book."

"Just you. You're a good test case Paul."

"You're not going to see the Dali Llama?"

"Why would I see him?"

"Pema" (Pema Chodron)

"Why would I see her?"

"They might have some insights."

"Would it be different than mine? It would come from a different angle, but for the purposes of study, and for the purposes of finding out what is true . . . I mean is it true that there is this thing called enlightenment or the kingdom of heaven or nirvana? Is it really true, or is it just as the communists say an 'opiate for the mind' so that you would spend your energy on something other than . . . who knows . . . masturbation and manual labor. (laughs)

"One of the Chilean miners is gonna 'fess up . . .'"

"(still laughing) About what?"

"Masturbation during the thing . . ." (more laughter)

"I doubt it. That's the last thing people want to confess to. So, anyway, What is it about being depressed and not being happy? You know, I kind of understand it because I watch my own mind and it's . . . it's full of crap. There's a lot of stuff in there that . . . it comes up."

"There he is . . . Eckhart says 95% of what we think is garbage."

"That's right. So, I'm examining this stream of thought . . . It's like constant vigilance is required because it's constantly giving me information and emotions that I have to either go with or reject. And the ones I reject are the ones that are, like negative . . . they don't feel good. How do we know they don't feel good?

"You feel 'em."

"Right, it's direct. Nobody has to tell you anything about a feeling. In yoga they say there are three ways to know the truth. The first is direct perception. That's what we use to process thoughts and emotions. Then there is inference. That's what science is all about; collecting observations and making inferences that may prove to be true. I think it would be an inference to say that we know it's gonna get dark outside because we live on this spinning planet near a bright fiery star and we alternately get periods of light and dark. Is that an inference? I won't perceive it until it gets dark, but I know it's gonna get dark. It always does. I guess we could make a big deal of the nature of inferences . . ."

"What's the third way?"

"I thought you'd never ask. Last is the 'testimony of the enlightened'. That would be the 'Word of God' or the statements of the Buddha and other religious heavies. But, you know, it's not like I want to write a book and get it published. That's not the object. The object is just to be here with an idea and to go into it; to see if the intuition sustains itself with inspiration."

"What about communicating with other people?"

"Maybe it will actually become a book. But, to have ambition . . . I don't know if that's as important. I mean you can't avoid it, can you? Maybe you can! You've got to think like that because you're in a time bound situation. Right? And there's like meeting the physical necessities and that's an important thing. You know?

"Indubitably . . . Yeah"

"But more important than that Paul, more important than that . . . and this is what we've been talking about, is the whole idea of 'story' versus reality or life. Because who are we and what are we really doing? That's the important thing. If a book could possibly communicate that, then it would be valuable. It's not valuable as entertainment like Eckhart says. It is entertaining to uncover who you are. It's infinitely entertaining to uncover who you are because it's a delightful process if it can be presented in a way that can be understood. And, the way it is understood best is by intuition. Because all the teachings that have ever happened, in any religion, have approached the Ultimate Reality of the human being who hears the teaching in a way to produce a result called . . . whatever . . . cosmic consciousness, the kingdom of heaven, nirvana, etcetera.

There is a result that is aimed at. But, the aim is an intuitive aim, and the receiving is an intuitive receiving. And this Ultimate Reality is not something that can be put into words or handled with thought effectively. It can only be handled by being itself. And being itself can only be perceived by intuition. So, intuition is, really, the key to the whole thing. And so, the book would be about 'What is intuition?' and 'How do I develop it?' How can I recognize it in myself.' 'What does it do for me?" How can I use intuition to study existence; especially in this world vis a vis all the problems . . . you know? . . . 'How can I use the key of intuition to produce a result . . . a reality . . . that negates the problems of the world? Like Jesus said "I have overcome the world." What did he mean? He meant he doesn't have to deal with the world. He's not from the world. He's from the land of intuition, the land of 'I Amness.' . . . see . . . And we're all from the land of 'I Amness' which is what this 'new age' thing is all about. The categories of thought, religions, other 'isms', all the attempts to be something in the world are going to go by the wayside in the light of this new understanding of who we are. It's just going to happen. This book could potentially help that process if we remain in our intuitive state; what is called 'presence' by many spiritual teachers. All we have to do is hold that light and make our best attempts to discuss what that is. And, by itself, that light will produce the result that it wants."

"Have you ever . . . uh . . . googled 'intuition' or looked at 'Amazon' to see what's around?"

(laughs)"That's a good question . . . well, no and I'm not interested. Maybe I should be but right now I'm not. Because 'what is' is so rivetingly fulfilling that I don't need to know what anybody else thinks. The universe puts me where I am . . . . and says sing . . . I say.well, what song? It says sing the song I give you . . . well, what song is that? It's the song of intuition . . . well, what does it intuit? It intuits love. It intuits what is now. It doesn't need anything from outside. It is complete unto itself . . . see . . . And that's what people are looking for. They're looking for presence; the simple presence of being: all there ever is. They *think* they need something from outside like more information or a situation that's better, a partner or money. The fact is they *think* they need something. But they can't get *anything* without the grace of this presence which is always here and now. Thought is leading astray because it has no intuition in its lucubration. So, we may as well be aware of this presence, this 'I Am' presence; because that's the fulfillment of the entire aim of existence . . . see . . . Now once people get hip to this everything will change.

Everything. And that's the cataclysmic 'New Age' that' was promised by "Aquarius' and all the 'free thinking' from the 60's . . . you know . . . Eckhart Tolle writes about it and it's foretold by Jesus in his ministry and in the Revelations. So as this awareness of presence gains momentum, as it is doing, everyone is going to start singing the same song which will become a beautiful chorus in the world; like John Lennon's 'Imagine', one mind at a time, aligning itself with presence. It changes everything by never changing. It's the 100 monkeys' scenario. And it's unavoidable; unavoidable and totally desirable."

"Do you get a sense that people are seeing this?"

"Well, . . . do you see it?"

"I'm not sure"

"If you see it you will be real sure. In fact, it's the definition of 'surety'. It can't be doubted because of its nature. That's the beauty of it. The beauty of it is life itself. Jesus said "I am the life". When your attention is present and receives what life's message is, intuitively; not with thought, inspiration occurs. Thought can't receive. Thought can only 'push away'. Can you see that? Thought forms its 'own thing' and pushes that against Reality. Thought is like a creative process but in order to be truly creative it requires the background presence of life which is thoughtless; intuitive. Thought without presence opposes the flow of being. We can't get who we are until we receive the gift that is always present. Then the outflow of thought aligns itself with that being; just like a compass needle pointing to magnetic north. It's very natural. The fact that most people don't do it is astounding. The result of non-alignment is suffering, as the Buddha puts it.

Among yogis it's said that as we move to the far end of the evolutionary cycle of human being, men are only able to perceive the physical body, and that it, almost unavoidably, becomes the only existent reality. The body is the most unreal thing! That's the disaster. That's the 'fall of man' from grace. That's where death enters. Death becomes real when we lose contact with awareness of being as primary reality; prior to thinking. All the religions are ritualizations of the attempt to 'bring back' the original state of connectedness with what is. That's all they were designed to do by their founders. Of course it mostly gets lost in thinking about it rather than feeling its presence."

"Does this go for AA too?"

"12 step programs have done away with ritual pretty much. They stick to the topic of recovery and are therefore effective in saving life! What is the 'spirit' in a spiritual program if not connectedness with a higher power; a higher power whose presence must be intuited in the here and now if the addict is to avoid drinking or dosing himself to death. What is that? It can't be answered with the mind.

It can only be answered by the heart. And, the heart's knowledge is by intuition."

"On a scale of one to ten how serious are you about doing this?"

"I'm doing it now."

INTUITION AND THE NEW AGE

The 'What' of It

What is intuition? Most people who pick up a book with this title already have developed noticeable intuition. How do I know that? Life teaches what it is by its own nature. The only reason to talk about something like this is to clarify what is dark and to bring light or levity to the process of living.

I don't need to tell anyone that we live in a dark time and without getting philosophical about it there is pain and suffering in all of us. The growth of intuition is the way to see the value of what occurs in a way that can't be foreseen, planned or understood by thought. My background is in yoga and I was lucky enough to have been taught by a guru from a young age but I don't want anyone with a bias to be put off by my tendency to come from that model. Everything I say should be understandable and verifiable by ordinary living. The tendency of the ego is to make itself special with its particular and 'unique' story about its life. We all have an ego in order to participate in living and it must be noted that most of our troubles come from assumptions made from the point of view of the ego or sense of personal self. Intuition, as it grows or when we become more aware of its presence, breaks the stream of personal assumptions about what is true and provides a means of seeing with the common sense light of consciousness. Then the intelligence that lives in our being and is never owned by an individual in any unique way, can reveal the way to end suffering and produce what are called in Christianity the 'fruits of the spirit'; peace, joy, love, self control, cooperation and coordination of life events.

So what is it? I could say it in a million different ways but none of them would be intuition. Intuition is what exists in the absence of thought. 'Mind' and specifically 'human mind' is the awareness of consciousness. Typically, people want something they name to have content but 'mind 'is never content. When mind has content that content is in the form of images or thoughts or some subtle form of sensation. Patanjali says that mind with content is either awake or dreaming and that without content it is asleep. Mind is a sense organ in its ultimate reality. Who is the perceiver of mind?

The question itself is the meditation. It opens and does not close with thought. The questioning mind is aware as intuition. Inevitably, a stream of thinking will enter the stillness of the opening. Mind moves between these two poles. The words on this page are the current stream of thought in the open space of mind. Thought gives answers and intuition opens questions. Both are needed in the human mental process which generates understanding as the real life blood of why we're here in the first place; such a beautiful story.

Any problems in human living have to exist on the side of thought. Intuition is intelligence; still and therefore in touch with peace. Thought formulates information. Attention, the perceiver, sees both but due to the moving nature of thought, one needs to practice seeing intuition as primary because it never moves; it just is. It exists before thought starts which is why Jesus says "Before Abraham was I am". Identity shifts to its rightful place in consciousness and not in the time bound stream of thought. Buddhists call this 'crossing the stream'.

Most people notice only what moves and therefore they get out of balance. If thought is the only thing in the human mind that is moving, it is easy for thought to consider itself the only real thing. That is the root of the ego; the sense of separation and the beginning of a 'me'. It usurps the sense of existence or omnipresence that we are and puts it into a form of thought called 'me'. Consider the formula of Descartes: 'I think therefore I am.' This is the burden of the thinker.

Thought plays itself out as gravity because it concentrates the formless and contentless mind into thoughts. Thoughts are things and subject to gravity. It can get very heavy. Depression is the result of too much thought and not enough intuition of what is. Joy is what really is: pure unruffled perception of stillness; the alpha and omega of existence.

To understand what has been said up to this point, intuition has to be opened. This is the value of spiritual discourse. If talk comes from the intuition of mind it has an attractive force which draws the attention away from thought and into stillness in spite of the moving nature of thought. In this way consciousness makes itself present during the thought process. Words can never hold intuition. What 'is' can be understood only in the still presence of intuition. That is true understanding. It is something you are. You never have to receive it because it is your reality and true self. Only intuition can bring to absolute surety, without any doubt, our connectedness with ultimate reality or Life in its sacred sense; devoid of the clutter of thought.

Talk usually goes nowhere which tends to make people think that there is nothing; no absolute reality, no God, no enlightenment, no nirvana and not much beyond boring and mundane events. That is the nature of thought. Each one has a limited content and meaning. It is like blowing bubbles and never seeing that it is the air inside them that is required for their existence in the first place. The 'air' or breath if you will, of thought bubbles is mind or stillness of being. The limitation of thought moves in the stillness that is joy itself. And, if we can't recognize the joy of our very existence, we become the result of our thoughts; limited and grave.

Spiritual discourse or talking about 'what is' does the opposite. It opens intuition and allows attention to be in its own nature for a time. Stillness then begins to be felt in the body and the body responds in proportion to its intunement with the goodness of life. All of us are either in tune or out of tune with life in different ways and we are at different places with our understanding vis a vis thought, but we are one in the field of intuition.

So the common spiritual practice of all religions is to listen to words that open and intune the intuition to itself. When doctrines come in, intuition and the opening are lost in a thought process called 'meaning'. Everybody is searching for meaning and there is none beyond the nature of what is; Life itself. Jesus and all he taught can only be understood in this light. Everything Buddha taught points to the reality of life beyond the processing of human inquiry. It just is. 'Why?' just disturbs it.

In summation, intuition is presence of being or mind without thought, The thinker or ego can be taught to perceive its own source by placing attention on what is still or quiet in us. When attention moves to stillness a balance between thinking and awareness is created that results in joyful life. Religions are meant to teach intuition but rarely do it consciously.

INTUITION AND THE NEW AGE

The 'How' of It

When attention is placed on the stillness of mind the higher capacity of intuition makes itself known as the presence of being. Intuition is the fact of stillness and dwelling there with full attention stops the thinking mind. The state of stillness is the nirvana of the Buddhists and the 'Kingdom of Heaven' of Christians. It is the end point of yoga practice. As has already been stated and what can't be denied is the fact that our human culture is centered on thought and misses the balance provided by intuited knowledge. In order to develop awareness of intuition meditation is necessary. There may be other ways, but meditation or concentrated attention is at the heart of all practices that result in the intuition of what is.

In the beginning of practicing meditation we intuit that there is a fulfillment in store for us but the usual habits of the ego have us look for something to see or think; something to acquire. We know that what has been taught for thousands of years as the path to freedom is real.

That is a form of intuited knowledge. Then we search in meditation for fulfillment the same way we look in life for some outside situation or person to fulfill the sense that we need something or that there is somewhere to get to. This happens automatically because of the nature of what is habitual in us: the propensity to consider thought as the only real thing existing. This is ego.

The main problem with ego is that it never reaches peace. From infancy we have lived in a world that thinks and identifies itself with thought, which produces time and, without intuition, tedium. Ego by its limited nature in thought and identity as thought knows that it is not fulfilled because it is by nature a limitation. Instinctively it begins the life of desire. Who am I really? I know I'm not complete yet. Name, fame, fortune, glamour and sex are the aims of fulfillment in the egoic world.

The primary desire of ego is a desire for attention. Intuitively the ego knows that attention is the source of life and it wants not only your attention but the attention of everyone else. Meditation as time is tedium. The fulfillment of ego's goals fails and many people give up thinking 'this is a waste of time'. They are not ready. The meditator has to have a sense that something is already present that needs to be seen: the life of attention itself.

To practice stillness has been the way of the various 'spiritual' traditions that focus on meditation to develop awareness through intuition. Meditation is not so much a 'doing' as it is noticing awareness itself. When we notice that awareness precedes thought, we begin to realize that we are the awareness and that thought is an 'add on'. The awareness of awareness as identity is what the Buddha called 'enlightenment'. Christ calls this being 'born again'. There appears to be a process here but it is really more a seeing through what blocks intuition; thought and emotion.

Because we have been habitually trained to think by our entire civilization for generations, literally thousands of years; there is a lot to see through. History has incredible inertia in terms of thought and emotion traditionalized. We think we are our thoughts and that the only way to 'know oneself' is through thinking. To identify our self with thinking is called unconsciousness because we are not really aware of who we are as 'not content'. Do you see how there can be no ego or 'limited self' if there is no content to who you are? Intuition remains and is in touch with the source of our eternal identity. It has a higher access to intelligence than thinking and no desire comes from it. It is fulfillment by its very being.

When we are centered in intuition thought takes its rightful creative place. We begin to process the unconscious and suffering part of our being automatically because it is a painful burden. It is the 'hangover' from being identified with thought. I'll speak more about this when we address emotions.

Intuition begins the journey and intuition is the goal of all process. So meditation isn't really going anywhere or getting anywhere but redeeming what is unconscious or dark in our person by remaining in the presence of intuition which is the light of consciousness as understanding in this moment alone. Bad feelings, irritation, resentments, annoyance, complaint, arguing and all the violence of reactive thinking must be seen in the light of peace for what they are. Any arising emotions or thoughts one encounters in meditation are entirely natural. They result from thoughts and actions that were taken without the benefit of conscious intuition. All spiritual practices which use meditation as a means of producing the growth of conscious awareness need to teach the processing of thought and emotion.

Twelve step programs are especially designed this way. They have no agreed upon Deity but intuit the presence of a Higher Power expressing itself in each of its created beings in a personally understood way. Christianity has become traditionally unfocused because the goal is no longer clear in the doctrines and dogma. Buddhism makes this the main point of practice but traditionally again; the goal seems to be a point in time or something to be achieved in the future which is never intuition itself. Here and now is the only 'time' and process takes place from this intuitive center. When the intuitive center is awake everything works. The intuitive center has traditionally been called the heart. Everything must be seen in the heart as it occurs in order to produce transformation.

To see the heart of intuition we have to be aware of what is occurring in the here and now. The untrained mind has a tendency to focus on thought as the most important thing and thought is always about 'past' and 'future' which are really just ideas. There is also the felt presence of the physical body and sensation of other sense feelings such as balance. The sense of being is always present in the heart. Thoughts themselves can be positive or negative and the force of their movement causes emotion or disturbance in the intuitive center which is the heart. These emotions or sensitivities of thought, being more subtle, don't attract the attention as easily as thought and, as we said, attention is the key. Attention is the center of all personal being when intuited correctly.

So what is present right now? First, there is the body with senses and the space around the body containing things living and inanimate. That is the obvious scene but there is always the mind; either still or moving. If the mind is still there is no problem and intuition guides the moment. In intuition, the mind becomes a sense organ and can sense what exists in stillness; joy, peace and love. These energies are universal and the heart is attuned to their vibration.

If the mind is moving there is thought which takes the universal energy and makes forms of thought out of it. If conscious, intuitively aware of stillness, the mind creates thoughts which serve the oneness; or processes the universal good. If mind is not conscious or stuck in identification with thought, ego, it produces thoughts which have mixed content or negative content depending on the amount of intuition available to the particular ego. Sustained positive thought is rarely possible in egos. The down side or negative thoughts are inevitable because anything that is not stillness must move or develop as dialectic. Both polarities of the universal energy must express. The ego accepts negative thought as identity as easily as positive thoughts and attaches meaning to both. A story develops called "How my life is good and bad". Life is always good but personal stories about it usually have a lot of 'bad' in them.

This brings us to emotions. Emotions are universal energy currents moving in the body and sensed in certain areas of the body; principally the heart and solar plexus. These energies are the energies of stillness and they are balanced in the perfection of their being. They are called prana or chi in the east and Holy Spirit in the west. They are inseparable from what we have called mind. When sensed by intuition in their stillness they are joy itself or 'Ananda' which means bliss.

When these universal energies get disturbed by thought, they retain the positive or negative characteristics of those thoughts. They become feelings that linger in a field of mind and are either active in the now or 'sleeping' awaiting the circumstances where the thoughts that created them in the first place arise again. Thoughts can be triggered by outer circumstances, emotions that get associated with each other, or imagining something to be happening that isn't necessarily so (insomnia is a typical example). They can build on each other and get completely out of proportion to the original causal circumstance. Emotions can create thoughts that are out of proportion or have nothing to do with what happens as a matter of fact. Eckhart Tolle refers to 'emotional story making' as the main underpinning of all ego. Anyone who has examined the sequence of their emotions will attest to the endless nuanced nature of feelings; weak or strong, explosive or vaguely present, positive or negative and an endless mixing and combining of the energies. Watch. The ego is a dramatic commentary. It diminishes as we move toward concentration and stillness.

The awakened soul aligns thought with the resting energy of peace and the thoughts have peace as their center. Thought is secondary to the perception of peace. Its main purpose is to create solutions to physical needs. The unconscious soul mixes judgment of life, attachment to results of action and resistance to life circumstances in thought and emotion. Those thoughts and emotions become a personal narrative or story that we claim to be who we are. Happy thoughts bring happy emotions and unhappy thoughts bring unhappy emotions or suffering. I can be successful one day and a failure the next depending on the story I tell myself about me. These two, the happy and the sad, cannot be separated. Ego strengthens itself by desire for the good and resistance to whatever it calls bad. That becomes the up and down of the ego's story.

"I would've been rich but I made the wrong choices". "Everyone would've loved me if I wasn't so_____." (Let your ego fill the blank. Everyone has one.) Both these examples are of the sad sort. "If I try I'll overcome all my difficulties" is more hopeful. "She loves me and that's enough" and so on without end.

Thought, when it is identified as 'self' in the unawakened soul tends, like all energy forms, to dissipate and become more useless as it expands in our being. This type of thought easily becomes negative because there is no perception of peace to prevent its heavy and dead nature from being sensed by the intuition which is always present in the attentive field. The ego's story becomes unhappy and the body is drained of its delicate balancing energy. The body becomes weakened. Positive rested health is lost and illness can result. Rest can rebalance the thoughts but the tendency to negative thought becomes inevitable. There is no fulfillment to this sense of identity. Without peace I can never be or have enough. The thought bound ego takes on a manic movement as its reality. Life becomes a drama that is good and bad alternately. Every high is followed by a low and the lows increase as the body ages. Increasingly the body needs more rest to rebalance the emotions. In Christianity this is called eating from the tree of the knowledge of good and evil.

When we learn to think after infancy, we begin to identify our 'self' with thoughts about what happens and these thoughts have corresponding emotions that attach themselves to the story line. Children, by nature, are self absorbed and the personal story evolves as ego. And, as already been seen, these stories tend to become unhappy as they grow larger or longer. The thinking mind is a problem solving agency and in the absence of stillness problems appear as food for the thinking mind. Thinking mind looks for problems. Unhappiness becomes one of the thinking mind's favorite problems because it can't be solved. Thinking causes it and then tries to 'solve' it by more thinking. Until stillness is realized that process can't be interrupted. Mind is so caught up in itself that even when true freedom is offered it is ignored by ego. Just about anyone you talk to these days is going to tell you about a multitude of problems both personal and collective because that's all they know!

So meditation develops intuition for its own sake. This is the natural simple process of our own true nature with its creative positive force. As one sits upright in silence thoughts become slower because the body is still and breathing slows down. There is an intimate connection between breathing and thinking. Breath actually stirs the mental/emotional field (mind and heart) as an impetus to think. Meditators who practice regularly begin to observe the turning point of the breath. In that breathless stillness pure attention is revealed. That is intuition in actuality; pure consciousness without any sense objects.

Now if you still ask "What good does this do me?" it must be realized that spiritual discourse is not really retained in memory as it serves to open intuition. Memory is not needed in the now for anything but process and process is the aforesaid analyzing and problem solving flow of thought. When one becomes aware of pure consciousness, the power of observation is developed that can burn up thoughts and emotions that don't serve the peace and stillness of our being. This is what Jesus called 'separating the wheat from the chaff' or what produces peace from what disturbs peace. This process is spontaneous and, by necessity, doesn't include thinking. It opens with intuition.

When a meditator begins, the thoughts have the momentum of years and do not become still easily. As I said before, many people give up because their thoughts tell them to. If you understand that thought is not a problem but just a natural phenomenon, and you can accept whatever happens in 'sitting still', your intuition will open automatically and the way will progressively reveal itself. Seeing through the screen of thought reveals stillness which is the goal of meditation. Thought can be there but the witness is not engaged in the message.

Similarly, emotion, which is the smoke from the fire of thought, begins to attenuate as intuition awakens. Thoughts are like sparks which quickly go out but emotions, like smoke, can hang in the air of the soul for awhile and be the source of more thoughts that create similar emotions. A negative feedback loop begins. Positive feedback loops can only result from being here and now in the presence of what is still; attention or life itself. Joy or bliss exists when emotion and thought become still enough to allow them to shine through the clouds of unhappiness created by the personal story. As practice continues or deepens we begin to disarm the old emotions that are associated to what is unconscious or burdensome. The stories of who I think I am are seen to be false. Life is present. A lightness of being makes itself known. Who am I?

INTUITION AND THE NEW AGE

The Goal of It

The goal of any spiritual practice is freedom; freedom from the practice and freedom from the necessity of being anything or anyone aside from who we are. When attention is placed on itself the goal is realized.

In the previous two chapters I spoke about the 'what' and 'how' of it. When mind, which is not necessarily free, learns the language of freedom, it begins to use its native intelligence to unravel its own darkness and recognize itself as the light it was seeking in the process. So the process or practice of a spiritual discipline is, of course, not the goal. What awakens during the process is the recognition of life as freedom. The ego co-opts the practice and seeks to find ground in claiming an identity from the practice. I am a yogi or I am a Roman Catholic or whatever the mind tells itself it **thinks** it knows something essential about 'what is'. This is illusion because consciousness has no image and is therefore free not only of thought but of all thought structures such as opinion and self image which cause a sense of separateness we call the ego.

The ego is a necessary part of who we are as process but that is only half of the equation. The balancing aspect is consciousness without process; pure being. Between these two, being and becoming, the life of the liberated human flows. We are essentially consciousness but it finds the expression of itself as ego in pure love and freedom. The purpose of spiritual practice is to see the essential nature of life as what it really is. It is as it is.

Spiritual practice is a purification of the mind and heart by hearing the words of those that have been liberated and practicing those principles in all doing. Being needs no improvement and does not pass away in spite of what the ego knows as death. All things that come into this field of being will pass: bodies, ideas and universes. The being of life is without time and brings time into being as a dream of existence in waves of energy using space as the matrix of the dream. That's why Jesus said "I am the life". A statement of that magnitude should be given in all capitals as it is arguably the greatest statement of liberation that can be made.

The practice of seeing what is in the now brings about the evolution of forms which we call the future and what a bright future it is! In freeing oneself from the thinking mind by noticing the primacy of being, one begins to see the future as a thrill rather than a threat. The present now is always good because it contains no future. The principle forces of being act always in the now. Now is the only time when things actually occur and transformation can occur only here and now. Therefore the future is only an idea. If one is aware of consciousness as being as close to Source as one can be, without thinking, the realization comes that Source is the true and unknowable parent of us all: the Father/Mother God. No other reality is possible and one is standing on the rock of existence fully surrendered. At that point thinking surrenders its opposition to what is and living becomes cooperation with what is and a wonderful adventure. The outcomes of action no longer matter as all is in the hands of a mystery much greater than can be conjured by the flawed and frightened ego.

Living in freedom is reality for all of us. What is not free is the ego or sense of me in time. Since most of us consider ourselves to be this me there is not much freedom in our culture. Instead there is a compulsion to get what I think I need and to feed whatever self image the ego has conjured up as 'me'. All self images are false and are the unconscious stumbling blocks of relationships. Unless I see that I am consciousness acting in an eternal now I will invent the future to fit my needs as an ego. Others become enemies if they 'get in my way' or threaten my self image. This obvious or subtle principle of the ego is present even in enlightened people and can draw one back into unhappiness at any time.

Living in freedom as an act of nowness is recognized by the presence of joy rather than unhappiness. "By their fruits you will know them" said Jesus and joy is one main key. People acting in freedom love others and want to include everyone in the joy they feel. Fear drops out because there is no future in the now.

The ego needs a sense of separation in order to exist and will create future as a constant force in the now that renders the self temporary and separate from what it experiences. The self becomes an object in thought rather than an absolute awareness without thought to judge it. The energy dance of existence will move with the laws of thermodynamics or entropy. Anything that comes out of the living source will dance as form and return to the living source in the illusion of time. You as consciousness will never move into time except as thought. Man means 'that of God which thinks'. (A free translation from the Sanskrit). So who are you when there is absence of thought? You are free.

INTUITION AND THE NEW AGE

The 'Why' of it

I'm going to tell a story so don't believe much of this. My source for this story is a wide variety of scriptures, tales, other stories and the words of enlightened teachers. There is nothing new under the sun except packaging and I personally like to use a conceptual framework for thought.

The encapsulated teaching says that only God exists and that creation is a projection of material dreaming called universe or universal existence. When God says "Let there be Light" a duality is created that, if seen as a result (as reason would have it), forms a trinity. The Word that creates the Light is Christ or pure conscious noumenon. The force or energy of that same light is Ananda (bliss) or Holy Spirit: the conscious phenomenon which concatenates into the material atoms. These spiritual atoms are used by the Holy Spirit to embody fine life forces (plants) sense and movement forms (animals) and embodiment of pure consciousness as thought (man). This is a continuum of reality and divisions are purely thought inspired. Christ is all in all; "without Him was nothing made that was made".[1]

So man, as that of God which thinks is able, with attention, to reflect the image of God as consciousness (Christ) as the agent of God's own enjoyment of His creation. When man's attention goes into thought he eats from the tree of the knowledge of good and evil. When attention goes into pure consciousness (Christ) man becomes aware of his imageless nature and eats from the tree of life. "You shall know the truth and the truth will make you free"[2]. Love and freedom are the twin attributes of the aforesaid bliss or ecstasy. It has to be experienced directly. Consciousness itself is man's meeting point with God but it is usually crowded and obfuscated by thought. The statement "No man comes to the father except by me"[3] indicates this.

In the beginning man was aware of his nature as Christ or pure consciousness. As the universe evolves it goes through cycles of the vibration and fluctuation of energy. The cycle that brings about the new age or 'a new heaven and a new earth' is due, on this planet, to the location of our solar system as it moves alternately nearer or farther from the center of our galaxy. This testimony comes from

---

1   John 1:1
2   John 8:32
3   3.John 14:6

the Vedas and probably many other spiritual traditions among men.[4]

Fluctuations in the cosmic energies due to the movement of the solar system nearer or farther from the center of the galaxy affect man's ability to perceive or sense with the mind and body. The Vedas note four ages in the consciousness of man.[5] They are given the metallic names of gold, silver, bronze and iron. Man's consciousness, which includes perception of all energies in the living field of the body, is basically timeless because of God's eternal nature. The physical universe however, follows the rules of thermodynamics and therefore entropy which appears as a time bound sequence. God's nature will continue to appear as a mystery to man; the idea of change in the changeless is time and the idea of division in the indivisible is space. All this is the result of the word Aum or Amen[6]

When our sun is closest to the center of the galaxy, man is said to live in the Golden age. All of us are like Krishna or Jesus and man's heart is at the pinnacle of its purity in relation to his Creator. As the sun moves away from the center of the galaxy mans attention can move more easily toward the illusion of separate existence. This is called the darkness because it is the creation of God rather than God

---

4   Swami Shri Yukteswar, *Holy Science,* Los Angeles, Self Realization Fellowship Press, 1984, pp. 3-26.

5   Yukteswar, 11

6   Yukteswar, 23

Himself. The heart remains devoted to the Source and that age is called the Silver age or Treta Yuga.

As the sun reaches the farthest point from the center of the galaxy attention becomes more involved with the phenomenon of the senses and thinking mind. In the Bronze Age the condition of the heart remains steady and enlightened consciousness is still the norm among people. The tenor of life is peaceful and calm. The Vedas call this Dwapara yuga. The difference between the Age of Bronze and the Iron Age or Kali Yuga is the shift in conscious identity from awareness to being totally identified by thought as reality.

In Kali Yuga humans are completely separate from God because thought knows itself only in separateness; objectively. Thought usurps consciousness and builds a separate ego whose source is universal life and consciousness but the awareness of the presence of that life is lost and ego perceives life and consciousness as separate and individual. We think of ourselves as cut off from others and that we need to defend and care for the body and its needs completely independently. The 'I Am' remains as the source of identity but it is totally covered by thoughts about being less than that. There is no intuition of Source. Competition is taught to children from the earliest age and is never seen as the violence that it is. So, in the Iron Age the world belongs to Satan which means illusion. Humans have committed the original sin. Sin means missing the point of life: to be consciously connected with pure consciousness or Christ. It means that we take the illusion as real and the real as illusory.

There is a time sequence for all of this which is laid out on the Vedas and is associated with the position of stars in reference to the earth. Accordingly, the earth experienced the depth of Kali Yuga around 500 AD. The end of Kali Yuga was 1700AD.

As earth is moving closer to the center of the galaxy once more intuition of connectedness with universal oneness is returning. Humans are beginning to perceive the fine electricities of life as in the plant world. Attention can move more freely to its source in pure consciousness and experience by intuition the oneness of all living and inanimate things. The assumptions of the ego weaken and become exposed as the fallacies they are. It is a cataclysmic time characterized as apocalypse by religions and their fear based (egoistic) projections.

We are truly in the new age now but one must be here now in order to appreciate this fact. Being here now implies that mind is not creating time in the form of past and future. Most thought is about past or future and causes' ageing as one's story unfolds. Not that the body doesn't grow old and die but that you as eternal consciousness never age but experience and embody universal processes as they occur in God's dream. One can plan the future because to the mind the mind is real. The foundation is timelessness but the projection of universe as Mind (God's) occurs as dreaming force material which is time and space as has been mentioned before.

Not only is it the aim of living to be here now but because of the increasing power in the flow of attention to pure being without thought it is increasingly necessary to see that life's purpose is spiritual awakening. The thought based ego is the source of crisis after crisis until it wakes up to its source. Upon awakening, the ego can be used by the awakened soul to process pain consciously and speed the freeing of thought from bondage to itself or, put more simply, to free the individual from self absorption and produce the sense of connected omnipresence.

Whereas people had to meditate in caves during Kali Yuga to eliminate the distractions of thought and thought based ego culture, now Self Realization can occur more readily with less effort through meditation and proper teaching. Spontaneous enlightenment will occur to some without predisposition to a spiritual path and others will begin to learn the principles through personal spiritual practices which naturally require self knowledge or concentration.

Unless one is blessed with clairvoyance it is not possible to see what the new age looks like in terms of objective realities. The main point is to be aware in this moment of the being of pure consciousness or life here now using intuition: the highest sensitivity of human intelligence. Being open in the now means accepting what happens as if one had asked for it. The universe is arranged to benefit all it is as an out picturing of fulfillment in joy peace and love. As more souls see this their activities begin to form the new culture. Motives that are loving and not self aggrandizing create institutions and societies that mirror those values. The universe conforms to the vision of the dreamer. As we begin to reconnect with our source, inspiration to right action and activities occurs more readily. It is no longer important to change things or situations in the outer world because the thrill of processing individual darkness in the presence of joy produces humility: the quality God loves the most. The meek inherit the earth. We love each other and want each other to flourish and succeed in our endeavors.

At the time of this writing the preponderance of souls on the earth are still locked in the embrace of the ego but more and more people are turning to awakening as their life's purpose consciously. Desire to have specific outcomes or results which prove the existence of God are basically from the ego and I have tried to use terms which allow attention to see truth without the active opposition from the ego which knows only its own opinions. Let awareness dwell on itself periodically.

The ego is necessary to think and live in the world. The question is whether the ego is its own source of inspiration (fear and desire) or if there is awareness of pure being inspiring action. A fine distinction between these two exists and experienced teachers or gurus become necessary. Most religious traditions have teachings that were originally meant to help the follower to discover the source within by building intuition but egos, in most cases, control the motives of religious organizations and they have become inefficient at best.

Legitimate awakening shows in the way a person lives. "By their fruits you shall know them" says Jesus. An awakened person uses awareness to process consciously the darkness of illusion which is the conditioning or habits in the individual and in the society that fosters illusion. There is no real separation. Assumptions, fears and desires are the underpinnings of the ego and cannot be opposed but only seen for what they are. Simply by becoming aware of tendencies in oneself and the propensity to create illusion by the society of unawakened humans, those tendencies weaken and deactivate themselves automatically.

Most souls on earth have had multiple lifetimes on earth during the time of entrapment in body as the illusion of self. Desires for objective situations in the physical body get generated by the mind and emotions during physical life which creates a magnetic attraction for the soul and it has to return to the earth again and again like a rock dropped from your hand must fall to the ground. Did you ever wonder why the population of earth is increasing rapidly? Until the unconscious idea that the body is the most real thing is broken, the soul can't awaken to the only possible reality that exists: pure consciousness is the real source of who we are. The body is a result of that.

All the major religions have the teaching of being "twice born". It gets presented in different ways but it is there in all of them. Born first to parent bodies the soul is unawakened and dreams the dream of earthly life as a body. With the help of suffering and correct teachings one is then "born again" into the reality that not people but the universe itself as a totality, a oneness, is your true parent.

The new age is more than just an idea. When people begin to see that they are, in fact, intimately connected with one another and with the planet and cosmos there will be an entirely different motive in living than exists predominantly at the time of this writing. The success of one is the success of all. Giving is far more satisfying than needing. Supplying the needs of the body is easier in cooperation than in competition. Fear separates while peace draws together. Beginning to live in the now is beginning to live in the new age; the more the merrier.

All of us are here and now always. This is the timeless truth. Nothing is ever lost or gained in the universe but sleeping and waking are apparently at the heart of the human drama. To use consciousness without thought as identity by living in a timeless now we remove what is dark or unworthy in our lives. Placing the attention on awareness as life is all we can ever do. "I of myself can do nothing, the Father doeth the works"[7] says Jesus. The power of life in the now lives through us.

It can be called 'intuitively doing the next right thing'. To cooperate with this life by consciously choosing to do that which removes the blocks to the flow of peace love and joy is the true work of humans however they choose to organize the endeavor. This is life in the new age.

---

7   John 14:10

INTUITION AND THE NEW AGE

Summary

Realizing who we are is always enough. Life's circumstances are unpredictable for most of us but in developing intuition we learn to accept all things as opportunity. When our processing of thought and emotion becomes conscious we bring lightness or levity to what is otherwise a grave and serious matter: living.

We all have egos in order to participate in living but the ego is not really who we are. In order to see the source of who we are we need the minds highest capacity to develop: the intuition. Intuition is the guide one needs to find the peace and joy that is the very nature of life.

Intuition can be noticed best in the absence of thought. People seek out times of quiet to pray or meditate and these are the times when our intuition is most keen. Thought and intuition form a 'dialectic of mind'. Both are needed to have balanced living. Attention can be placed on intuition or thinking but tends to see only thinking unless it is trained to see intuition and thereby develop balance. Unbalanced living is the source of all our troubles in this world. An unbalanced mind is subject to depression.

With intuition talk becomes spiritual or conscious. In all religions and spiritual traditions people need to hear the words spoken about the ultimate truth of our living in order to move beyond the limitations of thought and its concomitant judgments. Talk without honesty can never have intuition as its base. Spiritual discourse implies the presence of intuition and attention on this stillness brings conscious awareness of the subtle stillness that opens into feelings of devotion and joy.

When attention is placed on the stillness of mind one can be said to be in meditation. Since the ego lives in thought and seeks attention, concentration on stillness is difficult in the beginning. With practice the attention opens into intuition and the depth of being and its peace and joy begins to be intuited by the meditator. Universal intelligence which is prior to thought opens in stillness.

With continued practice of meditation we begin to intuit that our true identity has no content and that we are actually completely free of the problems that arise in thought. Thinking forms the active pole of mind and is used for practical life in the body. Thought is always alert for a problem to solve and if we are our thoughts we become problem makers because that is what the thinker does.

We look for problems to solve. The life of a thinker is one continuous problem.

With the development of intuition balance occurs and thought takes its rightful place in our conscious understanding. The growth of intuition produces a feeling of unshakeable peace that becomes a firm foundation for conscious life. The problems that approach us due to the inertia of thought find intuitive solutions and the problems of the past; the tangle of thought and emotion that we call our personal history can be processed in the light of still intuition.

The awakening of intuition initiates the cleaning of the heart. People identified with thought think continuously and compulsively because their life appears to be a result of thinking. Any change in circumstances implies a change in thought and thought dictates circumstance. There is a lot of truth in this but a thinker doesn't realize that emotion also follows and, in turn, creates thought as well. These emotions remain in the heart when they are not consciously processed. Negative emotions and judgments darken and cloud the heart and unhappiness becomes the constant condition of a darkened heart. Since the heart is the center of intuition or stillness of the mind, meditation reveals in stillness how to drop the heaviness created by compulsive thought and see that the soul's being is always a source of serenity and joy.

When we see that we are not the result of our thoughts and emotions we can be said to be awake in the dream of thought. The balancing of thought and emotion by perception of stillness leads to seeing that there is no time except the present moment to enjoy life and that creating circumstance in which to enjoy life becomes unnecessary. What occurs, without the need to change it, reveals itself as benevolent and trust or faith in living develops. Of course thought will resist this development as it resists all developments it doesn't personally invite but that ego must be seen through in order to have lasting peace. The path of a spiritual person, one who wants to be clear about the nature of life, is just seeing what is without trying to change it. Intuition inspires to right action.

The goal of spiritual practice is freedom; freedom from identity as ego and freedom from the practice of seeing that. In unraveling the darkness of the heart in the light of intuition freedom makes itself known as the nature of attention. Most of us are egos because we develop that habit from childhood with a personal story about life as a body. Practice of meditation develops intuition which progressively reveals our identity as consciousness until we are free of the ego's dramatic commentary.

The sense of separate self is a necessary part of what is real but it is only half of what is needed for true freedom. The illusion of separateness must be balanced by the sense of omnipresence found in consciousness. The ego senses its incompleteness and seeks fulfillment in various ways which cannot ever be fulfilling. By following a spiritual path the goal of freedom, which implies conscious awareness of peace and joy, can be realized. The conundrum of spiritual paths is that they imply that there is time to do something. Being here now can never take time so practice is always examining what is in the now. Awareness of nowness is omnipresence.

How the ego sabotages the present moment with incessant insistence on future could be looked on as the crux of mankind's dilemma. The practice of meditation is to hone the sense of nowness in order to see this movement of mind into past and future. Intuition is our highest capacity to see as it does not exist as ego and is the connection point of the entire universe. So what's new?